ESTiMATiON

ESTIMATION

By CHARLES F. LINN
Illustrated by DON MADDEN

THOMAS Y. CROWELL COMPANY · NEW YORK

YOUNG MATH BOOKS
Edited by Dr. Max Beberman
Director of the Committee on School Mathematics Projects
University of Illinois

ESTIMATION
    by Charles F. Linn
STRAIGHT LINES, PARALLEL LINES, PERPENDICULAR LINES
    by Mannis Charosh

WEIGHING AND BALANCING
    by Jane Jonas Srivastava

WHAT IS SYMMETRY?
    by Mindel and Harry Sitomer

Copyright © 1970 by Charles F. Linn

Illustrations copyright © 1970 by Don Madden

Manufactured in the United States of America
L.C. Card 75-106574
ISBN 0-690-27027-5 (Library Edition 0-690-27028-3)
1   2   3   4   5   6   7   8   9   10

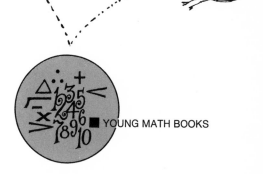

YOUNG MATH BOOKS

S uppose I asked you, "How many children are there in your class at school?" You could count them, and give me an *exact* answer.

But if I asked you, "How many people are there in your town or city?" you probably could not count them. You could tell me *about* how many people there are. That is, you could *estimate* the number of people who live in your town or city.

Or suppose I asked you how tall you are. You could measure your height, or you could ask a friend to measure you. If you or your friend measured carefully, you could give an almost exact answer to the question.

But if I asked you, "How high is the church nearest your home?" you probably could not measure it. You would have to guess—or estimate—how high it is.

An estimate is a careful guess. Many times, an estimate is good enough as an answer to such questions as "How many?" or "How high?" or "How far?" Of course your estimate must be a good one if your answer is to be helpful. Most people need a little practice to be good estimators.

Let's do some experiments. For the first experiment, you will need

 a measuring cup

and

a pitcher or
large pot,
        or
any large container that
will hold water.

Make a *careful* guess at how many cupfuls of water the pot or pitcher will hold.

Write down your guess.

ESTIMATED
CUPS: 50
REAL NUMBER
OF CUPS:
卌 |||

Now use the measuring cup to fill up the pot. (Be careful, of course, not to spill a lot of water and make a mess.) Keep count of how many cups you pour into the pot.

Compare your count with your estimate.

How good was your estimate?

Try the same experiment with a different pot or pitcher.

For a second experiment, try estimating height.

Look carefully at a ruler. Get an idea of how long "one foot" is.

Now estimate how many feet tall one of your friends is. Write down your guess. Then measure your friend.

How good was your estimate?

Estimate how tall your mother is.

Maybe your mother will tell you how tall she is.

Or you can measure how tall she is.

How good was your estimate?

Suppose the newspaper said:

"423 people live in the town of Turkey Hill."

"5,167 people live in the town of Beaver."

"About 1,000,000 people live in Houston."

Which of these is an estimate? About how many people live in Turkey Hill and Houston together?

About how many people live in your town or city?

About how many houses do you think there are in Turkey Hill? About how many houses do you think there are in Beaver? About how many houses do you think there are in Houston?

About how many television sets do you think there are in Beaver? About how many television sets do you think there are in your town or city?

About how many slices of bread do you think are eaten in your town in one day?

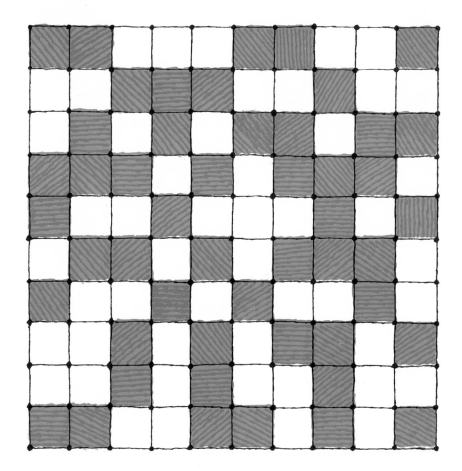

Look at the squared area at the top of this page. About what part of the squares are filled in?

Is it about one half? Or about one third? Or about one fourth?

Now count the squares and see how good your estimate was.

There is a story about a mathematician (a person whose job it is to do mathematics) who once asked some kindergarten children to say about how many raindrops would fall on New York City in a rainstorm. According to the story, the children said it would be a very large number. One of the children wrote a "1" with one hundred zeros after it on the blackboard. The number looks like this:

10000000000000000000000000000000000000000000000000000000000000000000000000000000000000000000000000000000

Mathematicians call this number a googol. The children decided that even in a very big rainstorm, the number of raindrops that would fall on New York City would be less than a googol.

Would you estimate that there are one hundred zeros in the number printed on this page? Or do you think you should count them?

You can find ways to practice estimating in your home. Here's one example. Try to guess about how many slices there are in a loaf of bread. Then count the slices in several loaves. How good was your estimate?

If you did a good job at estimating the number of slices in a loaf of bread, you may want to try a more difficult problem. You can also do this one at home.

About how many grains of rice are there in a one-pound box of rice?

What could you do to make your estimate better? (Without trying to count all the grains, of course.) Ask yourself these questions:

About how many grains of rice are there in a teaspoonful?

About how many grains of rice are there in a tablespoonful?

About how many tablespoons of rice are there in a one-pound box of rice?

About how many grains of rice are there in a three-pound box of rice?

Try to make up some other estimation experiments that you can do at home.

one
teaspoon

?

one
tablespoon

Rice
ONE
POUND

Rice
THREE
POUNDS

Or you can go outside and practice your estimating.

About how many steps would you take if you walked from your house to your friend's house? Is it "about 50," or "about 100," or "about 500," or "about 1,000," or "about 5,000"?

Or maybe you ride your bicycle to your friend's house.

While you are walking (or riding) to your friend's house, you can estimate how many leaves there are on a small tree. About how many leaves are there on a large tree?

Of course, if it is winter, it is easy to estimate the number of leaves.

Instead of going to your friend's house, you might walk to the store with your mother. Look around the store for ways you can practice estimating.

About how many loaves of bread are there in the store?

About how many people are there in the store?

About how many cans are there in the store? Compare one of the smallest cans with one of the largest cans. About how many small canfuls would it take to fill one of the large cans? How can you check to see how good your estimate is?

About how large is the store? You can get a
good estimate by "pacing off" the store. About how
long is your step? How many steps do you take to
walk the width, or the length, of the store?

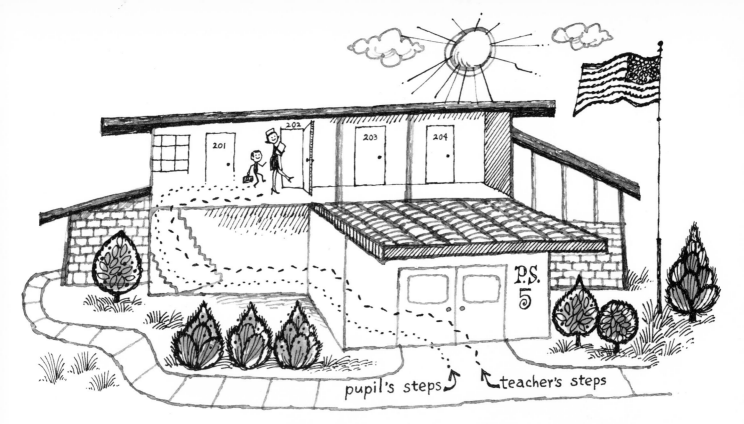

pupil's steps ↗   ↖ teacher's steps

You can also find ways to practice estimating at school.

About how far is it from your home to your school? About how many steps does it take you to walk from the door of the school to your classroom? About how many steps does your teacher take to walk from the door of the school to your classroom?

About how many children are there in your school? About how many teachers are there in your school?

Estimate how long and how wide your classroom is. Now measure your classroom. How good were your estimates?

Estimate how high your classroom is. Estimate how high your school is. If the painters are going to paint your classroom, they must estimate how large the room is, because they will need to know how much paint to buy.

Other people at your school must make good estimates. The person in charge of the cafeteria must estimate how many children are going to eat lunch. Then she has an idea of how much food to prepare. How can she get a good estimate of how many children are going to eat there today?

What other people at the school must make good estimates?

Many people use estimates in their work.

A builder estimates how much it will cost him to build a house. Then he knows about how much he will charge for the house.

He must estimate how much lumber and other materials he will need. He must estimate how much time it will take him and his helpers to build the house.

Why must his estimate be a good one?

A grocer must estimate about how much he will sell of different kinds of foods. This is very important, for meats and vegetables, and other foods, can spoil.

What happens if the grocer's estimate is too big? What happens if the grocer's estimate is too small?

The pilot of an airplane calls over his radio to the airport to tell the people there his "estimated time of arrival."

Why is this important?

If your mother is going to knit a sweater, she must estimate how much yarn she will need. Why must her estimate be a good one? What happens if her estimate is too big? What happens if her estimate is too small?

Each year the President of the United States must estimate how much money will be needed to run the country.

What happens if his estimate is not a good one?

Name some other people who must make estimates.

In what ways do you use estimates?

About how long would it take you to get into the house and wash your hands if your mother were to say: "Get into the house and wash your hands in one minute, and I'll give you a piece of cake"?

I hope you like cake.

ABOUT THE AUTHOR

"People have trouble estimating; seems as if we might as well start 'em young at it," writes Charles F. Linn to explain his interest in this subject. But it isn't really that simple. His interest in working with young children in mathematics is reflected in all aspects of his career. He not only teaches math, but he also works with prospective math teachers at Oswego State College in New York. Mr. Linn is the author of three books in various fields of mathematics.

Charles F. Linn lives near the campus in Oswego with his wife, Nancy, and their five children.

ABOUT THE ILLUSTRATOR

Don Madden has always loved animals and the outdoors. He is delighted, therefore, to be living in an old house in upstate New York with his wife, an artist also, his two children, and acres of wild country.

Mr. Madden attended the Philadelphia Museum College of Art on a full scholarship. Following graduation, he became a member of the faculty as an instructor in experimental drawing and design. The recipient of gold and silver medals at the Philadelphia Art Director's Club exhibitions, Mr. Madden's work has been selected for reproduction in the New York Art Director's Annual, in the international advertising art publication, *Graphis,* and in the Society of Illustrators Annual.